High Paying Jobs You Can Do From Home

A Guide to High Paying Jobs You Can Do While Home in Your Pajamas

© Copyright 2018 - Timothy Braxton - All rights reserved.

The content contained within this book may not be reproduced, duplicated or transmitted without direct written permission from the author or the publisher.

Under no circumstances will any blame or legal responsibility be held against the publisher, or author, for any damages, reparation, or monetary loss due to the information contained within this book. Either directly or indirectly.

Legal Notice:

This book is copyright protected. This book is only for personal use. You cannot amend, distribute, sell, use, quote or paraphrase any part, or the content within this book, without the consent of the author or publisher.

Disclaimer Notice:

Please note the information contained within this document is for educational and entertainment purposes only. All effort has been executed to present accurate, up to date, and reliable, complete information. No warranties of any kind are declared or implied. Readers acknowledge that the author is not engaging in the rendering of legal, financial, medical or professional advice. The content within this book has been derived from various sources. Please consult a licensed professional before attempting any techniques outlined in this book.

By reading this document, the reader agrees that under no circumstances is the author responsible for any losses, direct or indirect, which are incurred as a result of the use of information contained within this document, including, but not limited to, — errors, omissions, or inaccuracies.

Table Of Contents

Table Of Contents
Introduction
The World Is Fast Evolving
The Beauty in Working from the Comfort of Your Home
Chapter 1- Graphic Designers
Job Responsibilities
Salary Scale
Chapter 2- Public Relations Specialists
Job Responsibilities
Salary Scale
Chapter 3 - Executive Recruiter
Job Responsibilities
Salary Scale
Chapter 4 - Tax Preparers
Job Responsibilities
Salary Scale
Chapter 5 - Writer/Author
Job Responsibilities
Salary Scale
Chapter 6 - Market Researcher
Job Responsibilities
Salary Scale
Chapter 7 - Computer Software Engineer
Job Responsibilities
Salary Scale
Chapter 8 - Ethical Hacker
Job Responsibilities
Salary Scale

Chapter 9 - Financial Planner
Job Responsibilities
Salary Scale
Chapter 10 - Clinical Regulatory Affairs Directors
Job Responsibilities
Salary Scale
Chapter 11 - Physicians
Job Responsibilities
Salary Scale
Chapter 12 - Affiliate Marketers
Job Responsibilities
Salary Scale
Chapter 13 - Cloud Engineers
Job Responsibilities
Salary Scale
Chapter 14 - Corporate Counsel
Job Responsibilities
Salary Scale
Chapter 15 - Enterprise Architect
Job Responsibilities
Salary Scale
Conclusion
Let Technology Save You The Stress!
Plan Out Your Future

Introduction

You set the alarm for 5am and when it jolts you up you start your day full of work and stress, but what you hate most is the commute to and from work. You drive your car, ride the subway or catch different buses in a bid to start work early. Tired and stressed out, you continue your daily routine in a workspace with washed out and gloomy colors. Gradually you find yourself gazing longingly at the clock, waiting for the time to leave work. Every day at work seems harder than the previous, and you think to yourself, when will this end?

Let's paint another all-too-real scenario. College or high school is finally over! After a few years of college, the time you've been waiting for all your life is finally here, getting that dream job. Thoughts of the adventures you will have while working keep you awake at night. However, fantasies of penthouses and fat bonuses gently fade from your mind, as you find yourself jobless and unemployed months after leaving college. Better still you are under-employed, working for far less than your worth.

The World Is Fast Evolving

Let's face it, the job market is constantly changing. The influx of disruptive technologies like Artificial Intelligence, the Cloud, and Big data is shrinking opportunities for conventional office jobs. Hold on, all hope is not lost. The rise in technological innovations have given rise to freelancing - the freedom to choose your own working hours and to work from your own home - your comfort zone. Mobile technology has empowered so many people to accomplish tasks from home with limited supervision. For instance, IT analysts, statistical data analysts, graphic designers, and animators can practically work anywhere and with minimum supervision.

The Beauty in Working from the Comfort of Your Home

The gig economy is booming. In fact, freelancing is fast gaining much ground across various workforces. For instance, Payoneer, a leading financial platform, has estimated that the

American workforce will contain about 40 percent freelancers by 2020. Europe already boasts the largest number of freelancers, with Asia and Africa trailing closely behind. Working at home offers you flexibility - the ability to choose your working hours. It saves you the cost of commuting to and from your workplace. In addition to this, you also get to reduce your wardrobe allowance. What's more, working from home doesn't mean you have to lose out on high-paying jobs. According to Flexjobs, freelancing gigs are some of the highest paying jobs. Freelancing jobs like Data architect, animation, and Solutions architect can bring in income higher than $100,000 per year. So, to help to make the decision to break free from your time-consuming jobs, we've collected an amazing array of high-paying jobs that you can do from the comfort of your home. So, sit back, relax, and explore the rich opportunities we've brought to your kitchen table!

Chapter 1 - Graphic Designers

The phrase 'a picture says a thousand words', comes to life in the hands of a graphic designer. This job is fast becoming a major freelance niche, as we see 38 percent of graphic designers becoming freelancers. Graphic designers have mastered the ability to combine creativity with their artistic talent coupled with the use of technology to create images and texts for clients.

So, if you have knowledge of creative design and fine arts, then this is the right fit for you. From designing a small business logo to the creation of a branding package, this job covers it all. More so, graphic designing goes beyond print design. Web design is also an integral part of graphic design and it definitely ranks high in terms of income. It involves learning how to use web design tools and codes like HTML, XML, PHP, and other programming languages.

Job Responsibilities

Designing annual report covers, advertisements, books and their covers, logos, brochures, artwork, magazine covers, signs, stickers, web pages, tee shirts, and other branding and communication materials.

Communicating with clients to understand their preferences in order to create the desired design.

Tailoring a design portfolio to closely fit the client's budget and needs.

Pitching different ideas on how to actualize a client's project.

Creating a design by software, hands, painting or drawing to achieve the desired result.

Salary Scale

Just like any other creative, the salary scale in graphics design is determined by experience and skill level. For instance, salary.com estimates the income of freelance graphic designers with 5 to

10 years of experience at $71,000 or $34 per hour. For those less than five years of experience, the mean income can range from $40,000 to $57,000 with a mean rate of $24 per hour.

Chapter 2- Public Relations Specialists

If you have great interpersonal skills and can skillfully draft articles or press releases, this job is definitely what you need. Every organization out there undoubtedly requires the services of public relations specialists. Just name it - from religious to civic to government to educational institutions to even advertising organizations they all need your services. Mind you, this position is different from advertising since you don't need to pay for ad space in a publication or digital platform. Also known as communications managers, public relations specialists are the link between organizations and the general public.

Public relations specialist help shape the public's perception of the organization through press releases, media coverage, and arrange interviews for the organization's executives. In fact, many newspaper reports, radio and television releases are all generated from the table of public relations specialists. However, this position doesn't keep you restricted to your workplace. In fact, you can effectively carry out this job anywhere in the world. Be aware most industries require a bachelor's degree before you can get accepted for this position. Some companies require a bachelor's degree in journalism, mass communication, and literature.

Job Responsibilities

Write press releases and prepare information for the media platforms.

Help clients to convey their message to the public in the most appealing manner.

Reply to interview requests from the media and other platforms.

Arrange interviews and draft speeches for the organization's top executives.

Salary Scale

According to the Bureau of Labor Statistics, the average annual pay for public relations specialists is $51,000. However, the top percentile in this niche can earn as much as $101,000 dollars - that's a whopping sum of money, if you ask me. In addition to this, this occupation affords you the opportunity to handle different gigs simultaneously.

Chapter 3 - Executive Recruiter

Here's another high-paying job to add to your list. This position requires you to source competent candidates for a highly specialized position on behalf of your client's organization. Your client depends on your experience, negotiation skills, and your ability to draft job benefits and compensation. For this reason, you must have a deep understanding of the recruitment process and how to properly utilize recruiting software and Applicant Tracking System (ATS).

Yes, tech has made things easier, as it is easy for you to learn this recruiting software in order to get a feel for what this job entails. It's an added advantage if you have experience in human resources management and are well-versed in current market trends. Being an executive recruiter requires a lot of dedication and it will definitely take a huge chunk out of your time. It involves conducting multiple screenings and interviews for prospective employees on your clients' behalf. However, it is a flexible job position and you get to choose your working hours.

Job Responsibilities

Map out role criteria, document specification, and define position descriptions for each job placement.

Involves carrying out research in the market, client's company, and competitors.

Cooperate with clients to get their perspective on their financial objectives and hiring requirements.

Tracking down and identifying prospective clients via a variety of channels such as Applicant Tracking Systems (ATS).

Research and develop new hiring techniques and methods in order to get the best result.

Provide detailed profile summaries on short-listed candidates.

Organize confidential interviews and check credits and background information of interviewed candidates.

Salary Scale

Freelance executive recruiters are sometimes paid six-figures annual salaries. According to Zip recruiters, freelance executive recruiters get paid as much as $129,000 a year. However, the mean annual pay for freelance executive recruiters is estimated at $60,000 a year.

Chapter 4 - Tax Preparers

If you love working with numbers, this job will definitely pique your interest. Perhaps you have helped your family members or neighbors prepare and file their tax. Then, it's time to turn your passion into a high-paying job you can do from the comfort of your home. Tax preparers help clients to file and prepare their state and federal tax returns. Tax preparers must be familiar with various tax forms and the schedule of both the IRS and the State tax board. As a preparer, you are required to meet both state and federal licensure requirements.

These requirements often include a Preparer Tax Identification Number (PTIN), which is needed before you can receive payment for preparing tax returns for clients. Although this job doesn't require a specific educational qualification, you can enroll in different courses and training programs in order to get familiar with different aspects of tax returns. This includes filing status, standard deductions, dependents, wages, taxable benefits, income from interest, retirement plans and pensions, social security income, health savings accounts, business expenses, charitable contributions, and foreign tax.

Job Responsibilities

Using all appropriate deductions, credits, and adjustments to keep your clients taxes to a minimum.

Interview your client to gather financial information.

Compute overpaid or owed tax using calculators or computers, and complete entities on tax forms in tandem with tax tables and instructions.

Check data input and verify the total amount on tax forms prepared by others in order to verify the authenticity of the data entry.

Develop financial plans for clients and provide answers to their questions and complaints.

Explain state and federal law to individuals and companies.

Salary Scale

According to Pascale, the hourly rate for this position varies from $8.95 - $24.56. The annual pay also varies from $18,000 to $58,000 for the majority of tax preparers. Those in the 90th percentile can earn as much as $80,000 per annum.

Chapter 5 - Writer/Author

There's a large market for writers and authors in today's markets. Every day, companies and information agencies are looking for writers to produce content for them. Writing is quite an easy niche to penetrate. However, writers must establish their credibility with editors and readers before they can attract huge earnings. Writers and authors are mainly employed to develop written materials such as stories, advertisement copy for different online mediums, books, and online publications. Writing is a task that requires minimum supervision, and it's no surprise that about two-thirds of those in this profession are freelance writers.

Self-employed writers earn their living by selling their written content to magazines and book publishers, movies, theater producers, advertising agencies, and news organizations. An increasing number of freelance writers also produce written content for blogs and videos. You should know that there are different types of writers and authors. For instance, copywriters often work with clients to create advertisement copy and themes to promote sales and awareness. Novelists write books on fiction by creating fictional characters for an imaginary plot or real event. Generalists, on the other hand, have no specific niche and can write about any topic.

Job Responsibilities

Obtain authentic detail and factual information by conducting research.

Choose topics that will interest readers.

Work with clients and editors to bring the project to life.

Write fiction or nonfiction via novels, scripts, or biographies.

Present drafts to editors and clients for feedback.

Salary Scale

The median annual wage for freelance writers

and authors was estimated at $55,940. The lower 10 percent earned less than $27,000 while the higher percentage earned above $117,860 annually. In addition to this, the amount also varies for different niches.

Chapter 6 - Market Researcher

A career as a market researcher could be for you if you are confident, good with data analysis, and can handle huge amounts of communication from various respondents. Market researching is fast becoming a lucrative niche due to the huge demand for various market data by many companies. This data helps to shape company policies and gives them a competitive edge over their competitors. Therefore, market researchers are required to collect and analyze data and information on marketing trends, customer opinions, and investments to present to their clients.

Most market researchers are freelancers. This allows them to collect data for more than one company, thereby doubling or tripling their income in the process. As a market researcher, you will specialize in either quantitative or qualitative research. The former delivers faster results and it involves dealing with statistics and percentages. The latter, however, deals with providing the reasons behind certain percentages and involves analysis opinions. Qualitative analysis is a long process and might last for years.

Job Responsibilities

Formulating plans and pitches to present to the client or senior executives of an organization.

Planning different meetings and liaising with clients to negotiate and arrive at a consensus on different research projects.

Briefing interviewers and researchers

Hiring and liaising with survey groups.

Carrying out ethnographic research - studying people in their homes and other environments.

Using statistical software to manage and organize information.

Writing detailed reports on research carried out.

Offering professional advice to clients and management on how to properly utilize research findings.

Salary Scale

The salary scale of market researchers is based on experience and the type of research being carried out - quantitative or qualitative. According to popular job review site Glasgow, the average annual income of market researchers is estimated at $61,183 with an estimated average additional cash bonus of $6,403 per year.

Chapter 7 - Computer Software Engineer

This is undoubtedly one of the highest paying jobs you can do from the comfort of your home. It ensures flexible working hours and allows you the freedom of attempting other projects. Computer software engineers are employed in different industries and are responsible for writing and coding programs or providing an innovative software resource. As a software engineer, you will play an important role in the design, installation, and maintenance of software programs. However, having a basic knowledge of programming languages is a prerequisite.

Different jobs require the knowledge of specific programming languages. Therefore, you need to be comfortable with web-based programs like Ruby on rails, and traditional programs like Visual Basic and Java are also important. In addition to this, it's important to learn programming skills like C++, Smalltalk, Visual Basic, Oracle, Linux and .NET. PHP, in order to be part of the top earners in this niche.

Job Responsibilities

Develop and design software systems.

Presenting ideas for system improvement and reviewing current systems.

Maintenance of the system.

Knowledge of more than one programming language.

Preparation of training manuals for users.

Close collaboration with analysts, designers, and staff.

Salary Scale

According to Glassdoor, freelance computer software engineer salaries can range from $90,000 - $125,000 with an average annual pay of $105,920. When working for mega corporations like Google and Intel, your salary can be as much as $200,000 per year.

Chapter 8 - Ethical Hacker

Organizations and institutions alike are in dire need of ethical hackers. The rise in technological innovations has made it easy for hackers to gain access to confidential and sensitive information on company's servers. For this reason, ethical hackers are employed to protect computers and networks from unethical hackers who breach systems to gain access to sensitive information. Unlike unethical or blackhat hackers, ethical hackers aim to use their skills to discover any weakness in a network and patch it up once found.

This position involves simulating breaches to network security and searching for possible ways to overcome the obstacle. Therefore, an ethical hacker needs to have a bachelor's degree in network security or information technology. In addition to this, they must have good knowledge of Microsoft and Linux servers, Virtualization, and Cisco Network Switches.

Job Responsibilities

Must fix software vulnerabilities found in a computer system.

Perform daily tasks to verify security levels and the monitoring of incoming and outgoing data.

Reverse engineering of malware and viruses to determine threat levels to the system.

Responsible for the dissemination of security-related information to employees and company directors.

Salary Scale

Freelance ethical hackers are undeniably at the top of the list of high-earners. According to PayScale.com, ethical hackers earn an average annual income of $95,000. Sometimes, the salary can be as much as $150,000 per year. The U.S Bureau of Labor Statistics (BLS) indicates a rise in demand and salary scale of ethical hackers in the next few years.

Chapter 9 - Financial Planner

Most people are generally unaware of the countless ways they can put their money to good use rather than just saving it up in bank accounts. Therefore, they turn to financial planners to help them get the best investment and plans for their savings. Financial advisers are professionals who are well-versed in current market trends and good investment plans. They help their clients plan for their short- and life-time goals, from saving up for retirement to building a trust fund for future generations.

A financial planner can also give tax and insurance advice. It is no surprise to see why there's such a huge demand for financial planners. Financial planners are privy to the best investment products and services that are guaranteed to bring long-term benefits. Becoming a financial planner requires the ability to analyze financial information, a valid professional license, strong communication skills, and the ability to pay attention to detail.

Job Responsibilities

Ability to read data, recognize market trends, and predict the direction of the market in order to help their clients.

Must be likeable and trustworthy.

Strong communication skills and the ability to build trust with clients.

Recommend allocation of low-risk assets to clients.

Help clients to manage their finances regarding family and individual situations.

Salary Scale

According to the Bureau of Labor Statistics, the average annual salary for freelance financial advisers is $90,640. The top percentage of this profession earned at least $208,000 and the bottom ten percent earned less than $40,000.

Chapter 10 - Clinical Regulatory Affairs Directors

Skilled clinical regulatory affairs directors are highly paid professionals. Since they serve as a vital link as in safeguarding the health of people all around the world, they are highly valued in several industries, from pharmaceuticals to food and nutrition to cosmetics to biopharmaceuticals. Yes, these professionals are in high demand and there are lots of vacancies. However, you will need to have the qualifications and experiences that employers are searching for. For instance, you are expected to have a degree in a life-science-related field of study.

In addition to this, candidates with a pharmacy degree are more highly valued than others in this position. You must also possess problem-solving skills, presentation skills, time management skills, and negotiation skills in order to get the desired results. Clinical regulatory affairs directors oversee supervising the process of getting through clinical trials and into the market. They also act as a liaison between drug and food regulatory bodies and their companies. Therefore, the success of the company indirectly hinges on their ability to get the product approved.

Job Responsibilities

Handle both short- and long-term planning of regulatory submission protocols.

Provide guidance and manage regulatory teams.

Solve important regulatory issues by negotiating with external agencies.

Ensure approval of products and services.

Prepare and submit applications and reports on new strategies.

Train and supervise regulatory staffs.

Coordinate and organize product packages for regulatory submissions in tandem with the Food and Drug Administration or any other regulatory body.

Monitor and incorporate new federal and international registration requirements by reviewing various publications.

Salary Scale

According to The U.S. Bureau of Labor Statistics (BLS), Clinical regulatory affairs directors are amongst the highest in the "manager" and niche in employment statistics. PayScale places the average income for Clinical regulatory affairs directors at $96,891, which is close to the six-figure mark.

Chapter 11 - Physicians

Unbelievable, right? Yes, thanks to the massive strides in technology, physicians can now work from the comfort of their home and can even dictate their own working hours. Through the use of telemedicine, physicians can use digital tools like text-based chatting and video calling to discuss symptoms with their patients, recommend drugs, and provide preliminary care. In fact, this new branch of administering to patients is fast gaining ground as it reduces the congestion in hospitals and the time wasted while waiting for an appointment. As a freelance physician, you can earn much more money than when you work different shifts at the hospital. In addition to this, your patients will have immediate access to medical care without the need to wait for appointments. Mind you, the number of freelance physicians will increase as more hospitals are now adopting this new method of patient care.

Job Responsibilities

Carrying out routine checkups on patients to ascertain their health condition.

Assign periodic examinations on ill patients at a nearby hospital.

Give appropriate advice on health habits such as diet and hygiene.

Prescribe medications or drugs based on the patient's medical history.

Interpret lab results to gain an insight into underlying infections and abnormalities.

Collaborate with other medical personnel to form a high performing medical team.

Ask intuitive questions to get the root cause of illness or infection.

Cultivate an atmosphere of trust with the patient.

Remain up-to-date with recent developments in the medical field and other major niches.

Have a basic knowledge of how to use modern digital tools in order to work efficiently.

Salary Scale

The salary scale for freelance physicians varies greatly from region to region, and the difference might run into five figures. However, the National average for freelance doctors stands at $150,240. Sometimes, freelance physicians might earn as much as $280,000 depending on level of experience and field of specialization.

Chapter 12 - Affiliate Marketers

Affiliate marketing is undoubtedly a high-paying freelance job. It involves a partnership between a website or a sales organization such as Amazon and a marketer or a vendor. In this position, affiliate marketers help manage the relationship between their company and their affiliate partners to generate sales for their firm. This is a win-win profit-making model that enables both parties to make money based on different criteria that occur on the salesperson's website. This includes the number of clicks, transactions, and registrations.

Your job as an affiliate marketer revolves around planning and executing marketing programs to support and recruit new affiliate recruits. Some employers require one to three years of marketing experience. Don't worry if you are yet to acquire any experience or qualification for this position, as you can easily learn various online courses on digital and affiliate marketing. Candidates for this position should be proficient in Microsoft Office, cold-calling, and must possess analytical skills in reading market trends.

Job Responsibilities

Utilize database and analytical skills in generating market reports and maintaining campaign management applications.

Have basic knowledge of project management and strategic planning.

Experience in negotiating and purchasing pricing for various media, from website pop-up adverts to banners.

Proficient in Microsoft Office and other related skills.

Salary Scale

According to a report from PayScale, the average annual income for an online marketing manager varies from $38,931 to $63,636. In addition to this the average bonus fell within the range of

$1,221 and $8,199. Mind you, the salary scale for affiliate marketing managers differs based on experience, region, education level, and company size.

Chapter 13 - Cloud Engineers

Big Data and Cloud storage are some of the disruptive technologies that are revolutionizing the tech industries. Many companies are now adopting cloud computing systems, since it doesn't take up space and can be accessed anywhere and anytime. Since this is a budding area of specialization, there's a high demand for cloud engineers in today's industries. Cloud engineers help to maintain cloud storage systems. This work involves lots of programming.

Therefore, cloud engineers should have a core knowledge of technical computer programming and hardware components. In addition to this, they are responsible for identifying potential problems or weakness in a computer system. They continually upgrade hardware and software systems in order to ensure optimum performance. Although their objective is to continually improve existing systems so that they aren't compromised, cloud engineers are also required to put plans in place, to deal with future emergencies

Job Responsibilities

Collaborate with software engineers and professionals

Recruit, train, and direct new recruits in the department.

Great communication skills in order to effectively address issues.

Provide proper documentation of all activities concerning the cloud storage system.

Use technical knowledge and programming skills to recover data, and provide solutions to system problems.

Salary Scale

There are no individual listings for the salary scale of cloud engineers in The Bureau of Labor Statistics (BLS). According to Glassdoor, the average annual income of cloud engineers is $75,253.

Chapter 14 - Corporate Counsel

Corporate counsels are lawyers who work solely for a single organization or business. These lawyers provide both legal advice and protection for their employer. The best perk about this job is that you can comfortably work from your home or anywhere and it has flexible work rates. You don't have to worry about an 9 to 5 routine. In addition to this, you get to earn a six-figure income from the comfort of your own home - how amazing is that?

Mind you, corporate counsels must always be in constant communication with their employer as legal cases can come at any time. To be a corporate counsel, you must have earned a Juris Doctor and passed a state bar exam. Most employers often prefer those who have studied corporate law. Candidates for this position must have strong negotiation and communication skills. They must be able to effectively broker deals and communicate with others at all levels of the organization.

Job Responsibilities

Offering counsel on a myriad of legal issues.

Writing, executing, and negotiating contracts and agreements on behalf of the client.

Review marketing and advertising materials to make sure they are in compliance with legal requirements.

Advise on legal liabilities, legal risks, and contract status associated with different deals.

Work closely with other departments in the company.

Provide training on legal topics to the employees.

Salary Scale

According to the Bureau of Labor Statistics, this job is projected to experience a 6 percent growth in demand, and this will lead to a rise in income. The average annual income of corporate counsels stands at $115,820 for all lawyers in this position.

Chapter 15 - Enterprise Architect

Enterprise architects are an integral part of large corporations. They effectively combine information technologies with the specific business strategy of the company. Therefore, this position requires extensive knowledge of information technology and business strategy. It's no surprise that employers prefer candidates with an MBA along with certifications and training programs in IT. Enterprise architects work with stakeholders and issue their reports to C-level executives like the Chief Information Officer. They help to control the way organizations invest in technologies.

In addition to this, they help to link the company's processes and strategy with information technology. Sometimes, the enterprise architect is usually in charge of work teams, hence, they must have good leadership and communication skills. Furthermore, this job requires about ten to fifteen years of work experience in fields related to information technology and management. The best way to start this career is to have a foundational degree in information technology.

Job Responsibilities

Align Information Technology and planning processes with a company's goals.

Endorse shared infrastructure and application to reduce the overall cost of operations.

Manage risks related to information assets and IT.

Upgrade employee skills and knowledge in certain aspects of operations.

Collaborate with business analysts to tailor business strategies with information technology.

Salary Scale

According to PayScale, the average annual income of an enterprise architect is estimated at $124,641.

Conclusion

No more rigid work schedules, no more doodling or idling away until you leave your office. This time around, you get to choose your work environment. You get to work at your own pace and avoid all the stress that comes from working in a toxic environment. Freelancing has infused every corner of our modern society. Scared of working alone at home? There are different platforms that allow to you to share workspace with others. The crux of it all is that you get to design your workspace to your taste.

Let Technology Save You The Stress!

Thanks to the giant strides in technological advancements, you can easily attempt any job from the comfort of your home, without worrying about rigid work schedules or an overbearing boss, although some of the above-named freelance jobs might require lots of collaboration and periodic appearances in workspaces. However, you save a lot on commuting, wardrobe, and unnecessary expenses with freelancing - how awesome is that?

Plan Out Your Future

Heck! You can even decide to give yourself a lengthy vacation with your friends and family. What's more, you stand to gain just as much as you would if you were a full-time employee. Although most freelance options comes with pros, such as the absence of insurance and health benefits, you can effectively plan out your finances to cover lapses. Remember, live and explore. So, take the step today if you've been contemplating the world of freelancing!

www.ingramcontent.com/pod-product-compliance
Lightning Source LLC
Chambersburg PA
CBHW030513220526
45464CB00006B/2781